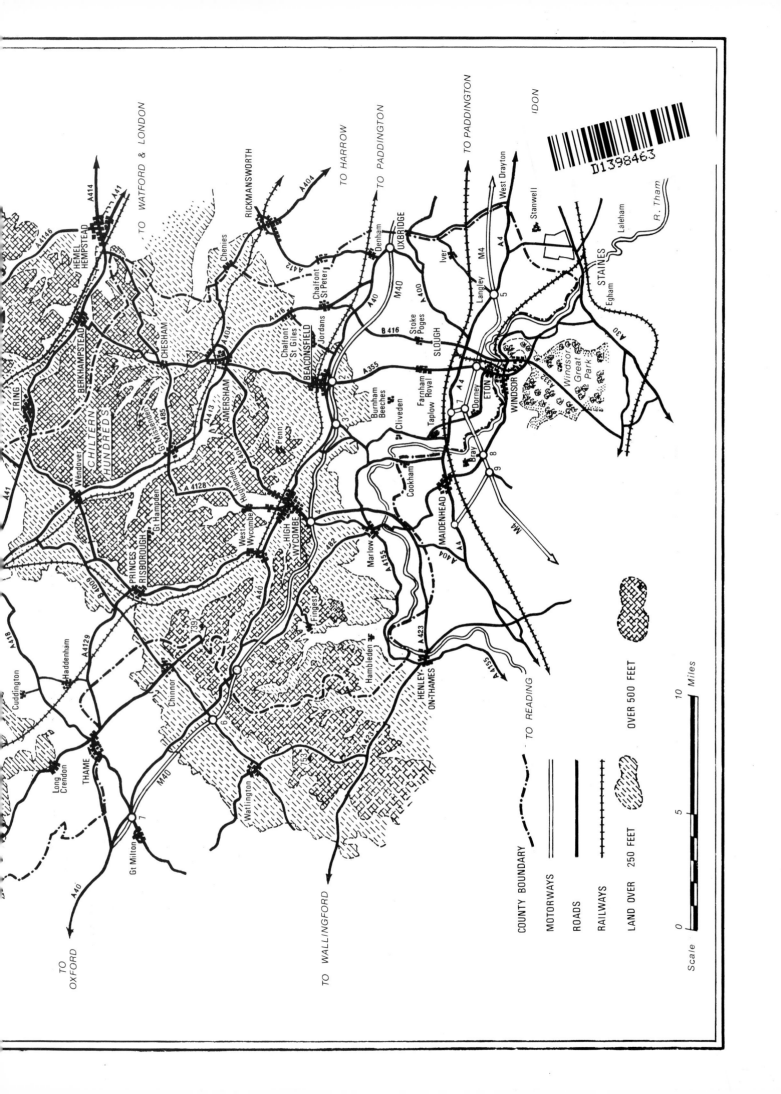

England in cameracolour
Buckinghamshire

England in cameracolour
Buckinghamshire

PHOTOGRAPHS BY JOHN BETHELL
TEXT BY ALAN HOLLINGSWORTH

Town &County BOOKS

LONDON

A member of the Ian Allan Group

Bibliography

The Buildings of England: Buckinghamshire, Nikolaus Pevsner; Penguin Books, 1960.

The King's England: Buckinghamshire, Arthur Mee; Hodder & Stoughton, 1940.

Regions of Britain: The Home Counties, Marcus Crouch; Robert Hale, 1975.

Shell County Guides: Buckinghamshire, Bruce Watkin; Faber & Faber, 1982.

First published 1984

ISBN 0 86364 022 2

Published by Town & County Books Ltd, Shepperton, Surrey;
and printed in Italy by
Graphische Betriebe Athesia, Bolzano

Introduction

The abiding appeal of Buckinghamshire is not just the beauty and variety of its landscape — all the Home Counties have that — but a pervasive and unique feeling of homely peace and comfort. Is there anything to match the stillness and beauty of beechwoods in high summer? The tranquility of gentle rolling hills, quiet slow streams and cattle standing knee-deep in water meadows? Or of mellow brick houses nestling along winding lanes? And despite the inevitable burden of London's overspill along its southern boundary, the county still retains its image of calm and comfort that was 'Paradise Regained' for the poet Milton and a vision of peace and happiness recalled in war by Rupert Brooke who loved the Chiltern Hills:

> Breathless, we flung us on the windy hill,
> Laughed in the sun, and kissed the lovely grass

Buckinghamshire is in area bigger than Surrey or Berkshire but appreciably smaller than Essex, Sussex or Kent. It has, however, the lowest population of all the counties bordering London although that population is now probably the fastest growing. Its irregular shape — Arthur Mee likens it to a rampant lion — stems from its origins as an Anglo-Saxon military district based on the fortified town of Buckingham and comprising 16 separate 'Hundreds' — family holdings whose shape and area had been determined by the vagaries of generations of inheritance and marriage settlement. Its creation was one of a series of defensive measures adopted by Edward the Elder (899-925AD), son of the cake-burning Alfred, against the advancing Danes whom he eventually drove back to the Humber. And it is, of course, from three of those 'Hundreds' — Stoke, Desborough and Burnham — that arose that 'office of profit under the Crown' in the Stewardship of the Chiltern Hundreds which since 1750 members of Parliament have sought as the only method of legitimately giving up their seats. In earlier times it was however far from being the convenient sinecure it is today. The thickly wooded Chilterns were the haunt of bands of unruly, rebellious men — some say they were Ancient Britons left behind by the tide of Roman and subsequent invasions. Perhaps it is to them, like all Celts they would have been natural dissenters, that Buckinghamshire has, as Benjamin Disraeli put it, 'Something in the air . . . favourable to political knowledge and vigour.' Certainly the county has been home to as sterling a crop of outstanding politicians as any county of its size. The greatest perhaps was John Hampden (d 1643) who challenged the king's authority outside the law and helped to precipitate the Civil War. There was John Wilkes (d 1797) the radical MP for Aylesbury and Edmund Burke (d 1797) the great libertarian and parliamentarian who represented Wendover and lived in Beaconsfield. The county has also produced three prime ministers: George Grenville who, inter alia, helped to lose the American colonies with his Stamp Act; his son, William Wyndham, who made amends by abolishing the slave trade; and the greatest of all, Benjamin Disraeli (d 1881) who was reared in the Chiltern Hundreds at Bradenham and was as radical a Tory as there has ever been. As with politicians, so too with poets: Milton of Horton and Chalfont St Giles; Gray of Stoke Poges; Cowper of Olney; Waller of Beaconsfield — and a claim to at least a part of Rupert Brooke whose joy was as much Lacey Green as it was Grantchester.

Like its neighbours around the London basin, Surrey, Sussex and Kent, Buckinghamshire has what the geologists call a 'scarpland' structure where clay vales alternate with limestone and sandstone hills running in bands southwest to northeast across the county. The major feature is the range of the Chiltern hills which divide the county in two and rise to over 800ft (244m). The Chilterns are the counterpart of the North Downs on the other side of the Thames valley and then the two ranges come together in west Berkshire. The Thames cuts through the gorge-like Goring Gap and goes on to provide the traditional southern boundary of Buckinghamshire until it is joined by the Colne. Travelling north from the Thames we have first the sands and clays of the river valley. Then comes the dipslope of the Chilterns, a tilted plateau where the chalk is covered by a mixture of clay with flints. Unlike the dipslope of the North Downs, however, the Chilterns plateau is cut through by a network of deep steep-sided dry valleys known as 'bottoms'. Most of them, like the Wendover and Princes Risborough 'gaps', were created by the overflow of a great melt water lake along the edge of the massive glacier that was part of the Great Eastern ice sheet during the last Ice Age and which extended as far south as Linslade and Whitchurch. The scarp face of Chilterns is remarkably smooth and unbroken with few chalk outlier's — another legacy of the melt water lake. Chiltern chalk comes in two forms: the lower is greenish brown, the upper pure white — a distinction that can be seen in the still vivid Lewknor-Stokenchurch cutting made for the M4 motorway on the county's western boundary. The lower slopes of the Chilterns support extensive woodlands of oak, hazel, fir and beech but alas the elms which once made up half the trees found north of the escarpment have all but gone — victims of Dutch elm disease. The upper slopes of the Chilterns have too thin a soil to support oaks but as Milton put it, are 'bosom'd high' in beech trees. And it is thanks largely to these vast standards of beech that Buckinghamshire has gained its image as 'leafy Bucks' and of enduring peace. For most of the year the interior of a beechwood is dark — beech leaves cut off three fifths of the sunlight — silent and still. Beech too gave the county its earliest industry, chair-making — or chair 'bodging' — in the Chiltern valleys. They may also have given it its name — 'boc' in Old English meant beech, hence 'the home of the beech', a more apt if less accurate version than the more generally accepted 'the home of Bocca's people'.

Along the north face of the Chilterns and following the contours of the foothills runs the Icknield Way, an ancient trackway that begins near Swindon and ends at Thetford in Norfolk. Some stretches especially along the 'lower' part have disappeared under metalled road but there are still long grassy tracks of the 'upper' way almost unchanged since prehistoric times. North again lies the great Vale of Aylesbury stretching from the Chilterns to the northern boundaries of the county along the edge of Northamptonshire's limestone hills. Not that the Vale is flat. Below the escarpment there is a belt of Gault clay which is flat and well watered. It stretches almost as far north as Haddenham, Aylesbury and Wing when it gives way to a narrow belt of Ampthill or Kimmeridge clay characterised by a series of low grassy hills created by residual deposits of greensand and gault clay over deposits of Portland or Purbeck limestone the farthest north this superb building stone is found. These hills do not form a continuous ridge as do the greensand hills of the Weald but comprise a series of 'outliers' taking their names from ancient settlements — Brill, Long Crendon, Waddesdon, Quainton, and Whitchurch. North of Buckingham in the valley of the Great Ouse as that river flows sinuously through Olney into Bedfordshire, the landscape is flat again and full of cosy villages and lush meadows.

Apart from its outcrops of Portland stone and the ubiquitous flint of the Chiltern ridge, Buckinghamshire has little stone suitable for building. It is, however, well endowed with clays suitable for brick and tile making both in the Thames valley area, on the Chiltern dipslope around Amersham and in the northeast of the county. All over the Chiltern plateau and the valleys running down to the Thames, red bricks and red tiles predominate although there are local variations — a browney red around Amersham and a silver grey vitrified brick in the southeast corner near Nettlebed.

These bricks are of the highest quality and many Chilterns houses houses of 18th century origin display pleasing variations of patterns and colours in their brickwork — diaper patterns — composed of square lozenge shapes — of red and blue bricks, contrasting quoins and carefully laid segmented window arches are examples to be found. Flint found in the 'pipes' and deposits of clay-with-flints in the region are also used for building usually in conjunction with brick. In Buckinghamshire, however, it was not usually the custom to 'knap' the flints into squared shapes as is done in Sussex and Kent but to choose naturally occurring flints suitable for the pattern or panel desired. The typical Chiltern cottage is a simple dwelling — brick quoins and door and window arches with a mixture of colours of brick surrounding panels of sparkling flints and all under a brown tiled roof.

In the northern part of the county, timber framing with brick infilling is the traditional style, the framing being regular square and undecorated. Frequently such houses were thatched — invariably in longstraw and with hipped roofs and a distinctive pattern of runners and spars just above the eaves. Thatch has nowadays largely been replaced with tiles although there is still a gratifying number of thatched cottages to be found in the area around Haddenham where 'wychert' — a cob-like mixture of clay and chalk — is used for the construction of cottages and barns and garden walls.

Pre-history's main legacy to the county is the Icknield Way which was in use for the transportation of goods from the southwest to east long before the Romans came. There are also several Iron Age forts along the Thames and in the Chilterns. The Romans left little other than roads although there are indications that there were several sizeable villas in the Chiltern valleys. Even the Saxons who founded the county left little that survived but much of their building would have been in wood. There are a few church windows and doorways of Saxon origin but the most lasting memorial is that curious earthwork known as 'Grims Ditch' that runs erratically across the Chilterns and was probably a boundary line. The Normans too built little in Buckinghamshire apart from a few churches like those at Fingest and Stewkley. Their defensive ring of castles around London — Guildford, Windsor, Wallingford, Berkhampstead — leapfrogged the thinly populated county and only minor 'motte and bailey' castles were built and have not endured. Indeed, the small population and the absence of large towns affected the architectural character of the county until the late 17th century. As a result there are no cathedrals, no major abbeys, few castles, no royal palaces and not many large churches. Little in fact to bring people into the county to disturb its tranquility.

A change came with the outbreak of the Civil War in 1642 which in part had its origins in Buckinghamshire. The king held Oxford and Cromwell had a base at Aylesbury so that much of west Buckinghamshire was part of the skirmish area and the scene of many minor encounters. One of the effects was to bring the attractions of the county to many land owners and would be landowners with the result that the Restoration in 1660 was followed by an upsurge in domestic building of the highest quality throughout the county from Bradenham in the south to Stowe and Winslow in the north. The trend continued into the Georgian era when the wealth and prosperity brought about by what we now call the 'Agricultural Revolution' saw the virtual rebuilding of many of Buckinghamshire's small towns and the proliferation of substantial houses everywhere. Improvements to the roads in the Regency period and the development of the stage coach saw the first beginnings of the outward movement of the more affluent Londoner along the turnpike roads to Oxford, Aylesbury and Stoney Stratford. But this movement was on a much smaller scale than occurred in Middlesex, Surrey or Kent and Buckinghamshire was to remain comparatively unaffected by the rapid expansion of the metropolis until well into the railway era. Although the Great Western reached High Wycombe in 1854 and Princes Risborough in 1862, this was a main line service and the GWR did not begin seriously canvassing for commuters until the end of the century when it sought the custom of 'those . . . in quest of a permanent residence away from the smoke and din of London but within convenient distance of the scene of their labours'. Then hard on the heels of the GWR came the Metropolitan Railway unique among railway companies of the time in that it had acquired vast areas of land adjacent to its lines and with it the power to grant building licences. Its creation from 1915 onwards was 'Metroland' — so beloved by Sir John Betjeman — and by 1933 it had set up thousands of homes in the area it served. It also encouraged walkers — 'hikers' they were then — and day trippers of every sort. Its motto was:

> *Hearts are lighter, eyes are brighter*
> *In Metroland, Metroland . . .*

The result was a substantial expansion in the population of railside Buckinghamshire and the creation of what were in effect new towns adjacent to the old and based on railway stations — 'New' Beaconsfield, 'Amersham-on-the-Hill', are examples. Happily — and despite the vociferous misgivings of the conservationists of the day — most of the 'Metroland' housing developments were sufficiently well designed and built to have mellowed into the landscape and created their own leafy tranquility. It is part of our national character that what was yesterday's eyesore has a habit of becoming today's treasure, hence the proliferation of a host of preservation societies. No doubt we can expect — in due time — for their number to include groups devoted to Milton Keynes and the motorway settlements of the county's periphery. Certainly of all counties, Buckinghamshire has demonstrated a facility for adapting to change that both Disraeli who saw change as inevitable and Edmund Burke who saw change as a means of conservation would surely have applauded. Perhaps it is something in the air.

Alan Hollingsworth

Eton College from the River Thames Eton College, Britain's biggest public school and possibly the best known school in the world, was founded by King Henry VI in a charter dated 11 October 1440 when he was just 20 years old. It was called 'The King's College of Our Lady of Eton besides Windsor' and its counterpart was King's College, Cambridge to which its pupils were intended to progress. Both were originally collegiate establishments — that is their function was as much religious as educational — based on massive and specially built churches. Eton Chapel — on the left of the photograph — was built of Caen stone specially brought up the Thames from London. Building was in two phases — 1449 to 1460 and from 1469 to c1475. The intervening period marks the Wars of the Roses and the deposing of Lancastrian King Henry VI by Yorkist King Edward IV in 1461. (Henry was murdered — some say martyred — in 1471.) Ironically it was Edward IV who built St George's Chapel in Windsor Castle whilst endeavouring to suppress Eton. He was unsuccessful but Eton Chapel never achieved the size and grandeur Henry had intended. Between the Chapel and the river lies Cloister Court built at the same time as the Chapel but of brick, a material not then used widely in England. The east range of the Cloister buildings has corner towers and numerous square stair and garderobe (ie privy) towers. The College garden is beneath the walls. When it was founded, Eton College comprised a provost, 10 fellows or lay priests, four clerks, six choristers and 24 scholars. In the 18th century it had about 500 pupils and nowadays it has nearly 1,200. Of these, 70 are 'King's Scholars' who live in the College itself and the rest are 'Oppidans' who live in masters' houses in the town of Eton.

Dorney Court, near Windsor The most enduring legend of Dorney Court is that it was here in the 17th century that the first pineapple to be grown in England was presented to Charles II. (It was was probably grown from cuttings imported from Barbados and they did not survive long.) The origin of the legend is obscure, neither Evelyn nor Pepys mentions the occasion. It is mostly based upon a painting by a little-known 17th century artist called Dancker which shows the royal gardener Rose making the presentation to his master against the background of a very large house said by contemporaries to be either Dorney Court as it was at the time or as its owner intended it would shortly be. The incident is also commemorated by a magnificent carved model of a pineapple in the great hall of Dorney Court. There is also a painting of another fruit that Charles II enjoyed — the loose and luscious Barbara Villiers, eventually made Duchess of Cleveland. She was married to Sir Roger Palmer of Dorney Court when in 1660 she began the liaison with the king — and not a few others, by all accounts.

The Palmers have lived at Dorney Court in direct father to son succession since 1628 when Sir James Palmer from Wingham in Kent married Martha Garrard whose family had bought the estate in 1555.

Although it has been frequently altered and repeatedly restored, Dorney Court has a well documented history going back to c1500 when it began life as an L-shaped hall house with the great hall in the longer arm and the solar and the parlour in the shorter. The great hall with its magnificent open roof, with thin arched braces, its linenfold panelling and its fireplace is largely unchanged. The east front, seen here, is a 20th century restoration of a Tudor style façade replacing an 18th century one.

10

The Kederminster Library, Langley Marish
A unique survival from a more religious age, the Kederminster library was established in 1613 when a grant was obtained from the Dean and Chapter of Windsor. Its books were intended for use by the clergy and comprise some 250 works in Latin including an illuminated 12th century manuscript, the 'Kederminster Gospels' which are on loan to the British Museum. The rest of the books are mainly theological works including those by Bunyan and Holinshead but there is one of Kederminster family herbal recipes intended to 'comfort and strengthen the heart'. The splendour of Sir John Kederminster's chapel is evident here by the magnificent frieze and overmantel which frames the Kederminster coat of arms. Just below the ceiling are a series of painted panels with landscape views of Windsor Castle and Eton College. Other painted panels — there are over 250 of them — are decorated with strapwork and cartouches, some with pictures of saints, others have illustrations of open books and are the doors of cupboards in which the actual books are kept.

In other churches in Jacobean times, it was usual for books to be chained to the desk. In the Kederminster library this was avoided — but just in case the clergy who used it were tempted, Sir John built a row of almshouses south of the church and required at least one person from them to be present in the library and not depart as long as anyone was reading there.

Bridgefoot House, Iver The River Colne, seen here in autumn spate, marks the boundary between Buckinghamshire and Greater London, Bridgefoot House is thus one of the first in the county and very typical of much of its traditional domestic architecture — early Georgian and brick built. It is of yellow brick with dressing in red brick — note the heavy segmented heads of the front windows and the aprons of the attic storey.

Iver itself is an historic village with a church — St Peter's — that dates back to Saxon times and contains a wealth of interesting monuments. In the 18th century Iver was the haunt of Alexander Pope and other writers of the day. In more recent times one of its nearby houses, Coppins, was for some time the home of the late Duchess of Kent and her family.

14

Gray's Monument, Stoke Poges

The curfew tolls the knell of parting day . . .

Thomas Gray, one of the best known poets in the English language, wrote his most celebrated poem in the shade of a yew tree in the Churchyard of Stoke Poges church. He sleeps now 'among the rude forefathers of the hamlet' in his mother's tomb under the chancel window, his own name and date of death — 1771 — unrecorded on the grave itself as his will required. (There is a later plaque on the opposite wall.) This massive sarcophagus was built in 1799 by William Penn's grandson John to a design by George III's architect, James Wyatt (d 1813). It stands just outside the church gate in what were formerly the grounds of Stoke Park (now the Golf Club) which was built for John Penn at the end of the 18th century during the period of the 'Greek Revival' when garden temples, colonnaded ruins and classic sarcophagi like this were highly fashionable as landscape embellishments. In consequence the landscape architect, Humphrey Repton, who laid out the grounds demolished a former rectory so that the monument could be seen from the house.

Thomas Gray was born in London but lived with an uncle in Burnham before going to Eton. Later his widowed mother and an aunt moved to West End cottage in Stoke Poges — it was later rebuilt as Stoke Court — and for much of his life Gray who was a university don divided his time between there and Cambridge.

Burnham Beeches Bucks at its leafiest...
The great stands of beech along the Chilterns give the county its leafy image and nowhere more than in the ever-popular Burnham Beeches just off the main road between Beaconsfield and Slough. The area of woodland, now about 600 acres, once stretched beyond Burnham to Taplow and the Thames. About half of the present area was bought by the City of London in 1879 and is still maintained by the City.

With its dense foliage the beech trees cuts off much of the light from the forest floor beneath it and in consequence, apart from clearings, there is a thick carpet of leaves with very little undergrowth. This in turn has given rise to flora and fauna particular to beech woods. Among the flowers to be found are the white helleborine and the bird's nest orchid. Many birds and small animals from titmice to grey squirrels thrive on the leaves, the leaf mould and on 'beech-mast' — triangular brown nuts that fall from the trees and which for centuries were valued as food for pigs. It is also reported from time to time that in parts of the Chilterns, near Wendover, there survives a small colony of a fat tailed edible dormouse called *'glis-glis'* which is believed to have been introduced for culinary purposes by the Romans. It is the only such colony in Britain although the animal is common in Southern Europe.

Cliveden Situated, as its name implies, on top of a cliff, Cliveden also commands a bend in the river to give it superb views along the wooded Thames valley as it winds north to Cookham. The present house was designed in 1850 by Sir Charles Barry, the architect of the Houses of Parliament, but the style here is Italianate rather than neo-Gothic and more reminiscent of 16th century Genoa than 19th century England. Barry's mansion was however not the first on the site. The original house was built by the Dutch architect William Winde in 1677-9 for Charles Villiers, the second Duke of Buckingham, the evil genius of Charles II's reign. The duke brought Lady Shrewsbury to his new home in 1668 after killing her husband in a duel. The duke died in 1687, 'worn to a thread with whoring' and in 1696 the estate was bought by Lord Orkney, the first ever British field marshal and one of Marlborough's generals at Blenheim. He enlarged the house by employing Thomas Archer to add colonnaded wings to it in about 1720 — the columns seen in the foreground here. The house was leased to Frederick, Prince of Wales and father of George III, from 1739 until his death in 1751 as a result of being struck by a tennis ball. He was hardly mourned —

Here lies Fred,
Who was alive and is dead
There is no more to be said.

It was however during his tenancy that Thomas Arne's *Rule Britannia* was first sung when in 1740 a masque by James Thomson was performed at Cliveden. The first house was destroyed by fire in 1795 and the house built to replace it was also burned down. The present house was built for the Duke of Sutherland, later passing into the hands of the Duke of Westminster who sold it to the American William Waldorf Astor in 1893. In the 1930s it was associated with the so-called 'Cliveden Set', — the name given to Nancy Astor MP and a group of friends who endeavoured to make peace with Hitler. In 1942 the Astors presented the estate to the National Trust and Cliveden itself is now, appropriately, let to Stanford University, California as a centre for European studies.

The grounds are open to the public between March and December.

Marlow One of the jewels of Thames-side Buckinghamshire, Great Marlow is now happily by-passed by road and has recovered some of the rural peace and charm that made it such an attractive place of residence in the 18th and 19th centuries. The poet Shelley and his wife Mary lived here — in a cottage in West Street — where Mary wrote her famous novel, *Frankenstein*, published in 1818. A few doors away their close friend, Thomas Love Peacock wrote his novel *Nightmare Abbey* and published it the same year. The coincidence of two horror stories being written — the one genuine, the other mock — has little to do with the place for 19th century Marlow was all that a lover of the 'picturesque' could desire and singularly lacking in Gothic castles. Shelley described it thus:

> Waterfalls leap among islands green
> Which framed for my lone boat a lone
> retreat . . .

(Shelley would be lucky nowadays to find himself in a lone boat. Marlow has no by-pass for river traffic.)

The photograph here is of the bridge and the church together making a scene which Arthur Mee called 'unforgettable and the best view of the town'. The suspension bridge spans 225ft and was built in 1831-5 to the design of William Tierney Clark who was responsible for the bridge over the Danube linking Buda with Pest. The church — All Saints — is 19th century but is on the site of an earlier building and contains many interesting monuments from earlier times. The nave was built in 1832 to designs by C. F. Inwood but the chancel and the spire are later additions, the one by Street in 1881-2 and the other by J. Oldrid Scott in 1898-9. Behind the church the tall house with the shaped gable is Old Bridge House, also Victorian.

Hambleden Village A typical flint and red brick Buckinghamshire village, and one of the most attractive in the county, Hambleden lies in a gentle valley with beech clad slopes running down to the Thames. The centre of the village is a triangular green with the church on one side and the gabled manor house on the other. The church, St Mary's, was originally Norman but its tower collapsed in 1703 and was rebuilt in traditional brick and flint in 1731. It suffered the inevitable 'improvement' in Victorian times when the tower was encased in cement. The Manor House, to the right of the church, is an early 17th century building and was the birthplace of the 7th Earl of Cardigan who led the famous charge of the Light Brigade at Balaclava (and gave his name to a woollen jacket). It is now the home of the Hambleden family, descendants of the first Viscount who as W. H. Smith (d 1891) bought the estate in 1871 and gave us a household and a high street name.

The large house on the edge of the woodland at the right of the photograph is the former rectory now known as Kendricks. Built in 1724, it is fronted in red and vitreous brick and boasts giant pilasters in the classical style. It stands on the site of the original manor house among whose early occupants as lords of the manor were the Clares whose name appears first on the Magna Carta. The old manor house was also the birthplace of the last English saint to be canonised before the Reformation, Thomas of Cantelupe, Bishop of Hereford.

24

The Hambleden Valley Typical of a number of small valleys — known as 'bottoms' — cutting into the dip slope of the Chilterns, the Hambleden Valley is about four miles long from its head near Fingest to the Thames at Mill End below Hambleden itself. Its sides are steep and rise to about 500ft (150m) in places and are well wooded with stands of beech, oak and yew which grow naturally and larch and conifers which have been planted. They all provide good cover for wild life of all varieties and even deer are frequently to be seen. There are also many game coverts and the map is dotted with 'Pheasants' Hills' and 'Pheasants' Woods'. As is evident from the photograph, this valley has been spared the ribbon developments and urban sprawl that characterises other valleys in south Bucks. This is in large part due to the generosity of landowners since World War II. Much of the land in the valley — 3,900 acres — and on both sides of the Thames was covenanted to the National Trust by the 3rd Viscount Hambleden in 1944 to protect Hambleden and Remenham villages. A further property — The Hyde, just across the valley from where this photograph was taken — was covenanted to the Trust by Mrs J. D. Coleridge in 1970.

St Bartholomew's Church, Fingest Its name in Old Danish is said to mean a meeting place and this mighty tower would certainly have provided that. The tower is, however, of Norman origin rather than Danish although, as Nikolaus Pevsner suggests in his *Buildings of England* it could have been built during the period of Saxon-Norman overlap — Norman work with a Saxon flavour. It has also been suggested that the tower may well at one time have served as a nave as Saxon towers sometimes did. The twin saddle back roof over the tower is much later and is believed to date from the 17th century.

A quaint old wedding custom is observed at St Bartholomew's. To be sure of being lucky in married life, the bridegroom is required to lift his bride over the church gate when leaving after the ceremony and the gate is ritually locked to ensure he does. In these liberated times, however, a marriage can still be lucky — at least as far as custom is concerned — if it is the bride who does the lifting.

Fingest itself lies in a deep beech-wooded Chiltern valley and has a number of Georgian and timber framed houses but has declined in size and importance since the 18th century.

28

West Wycombe, The Old Church and Mausoleum The church of St Laurence stands on top a commanding crest of the Chilterns 600ft above three converging valleys and overlooking the main High Wycombe to Oxford road. It is a medieval church and once served a village on the hilltop now long gone called Haveringdon. The church was refashioned in Georgian times, its tower was heightened and the great golden ball which is such a feature was added — it has seats and will hold 10 men. The purpose was, as a contemporary poet put it:

A temple built aloft in air
That serves for show and not for prayer

The poet was Charles Churchill (d 1764) who was a close associate of John Wilkes (d 1797) a notorious radical politician and pamphleteer who was twice expelled from the House of Commons for libel and obscene publications. Wilkes — he was at one time MP for Aylesbury — was a member of the Medmenham Abbey Fraternity also known as the Hell Fire Club who met at the Abbey which was leased by the club's founder, Sir Francis Dashwood. (The club met once or twice a year for a week or so of drinking and whoring and general abandon.) Sir Francis (d 1781) owned West Wycombe Park which he remodelled about 1750, refashioning the church at about the same time. He also built the odd hexagonal structure which stands in front of the church as a family mausoleum. It is entirely open to the sky and the three eastern sides have triumphal arches while the three western ones have niches for funerary urns in the best Greek revival style.

West Wycombe Village Screened by trees from both the house and the church, West Wycombe village was bought from the Dashwood family by the Royal Society of Arts in 1929 and transferred to the National Trust in 1934. It is a well preserved village with a pleasing variety of buildings ranging from the 15th to the 20th centuries and the Church Loft seen here is probably the gem of the village. Dating from the late 15th century it has a long first floor hall with an open roof that served in earlier times as a resting place for medieval travellers on their way from London to Oxford along the old main road outside. This refuge was provided by the church which is reached through the archway and a long stiff 600ft climb to the top of the hill. Another form of hospitality is provided by the old prison on the left of the archway and at one time local miscreants were manacled and flogged just outside. At the other end of the building is a kneeling stone beneath a niche that at one time held a crucifix.

32

High Wycombe, Market House   One of the busiest towns in the county, High Wycombe spreads some five miles along the floor of the valley of the little River Wye, its streets and houses climbing up the valley sides. It has been a market town for centuries and this Market Hall stands on the site of one which was built early in the 17th century. The present one was built by Robert Adam in 1761 and was presented to the town by the Shelburnes who then owned Wycombe Abbey. It is not usually regarded as one of Adams' masterpieces but it has a quaint charm of its own. The leaded dome and the lantern are late 19th century additions. Note the lettering on the stringcourse which gives 'To London 29 miles' on the southwest face and 'To Oxford 25 miles' on the southeast one.

High Wycombe, The Guildhall Another gift from Lord Shelburne, High Wycombe's Guildhall was built in 1757 and the architect was Henry Keene (d 1776) who was Surveyor to Westminster Abbey and an authority on Gothic architecture. He was also responsible for the tower of High Wycome's parish church of All Saints, 'a very pretty piece of early Gothic Revival' says Nikolaus Pevsner. But here he is in the neo-Classical mode — notice the particularly attractive cupola, its Tuscan colonnettes matching the Tuscan arcading of the groundfloor. Notice too the weather vane on the cupola — a centaur shooting an arrow into the wind. In a backroom at the Guildhall is a large painting by J. H. Mortimer (d 1779), a romantic artist well-known for his conversation pieces, the subject being 'St Paul converting the Druids'.

High Wycombe itself is renowned as a centre for furniture making which began as an outlet for the products of the local beech woods. In earlier times the initial turning and shaping of chair legs and rails was done in the woods by 'bodgers' — a possible origin of the word 'bodged' meaning incomplete and roughly done. But the bodgers have now gone and modern High Wycombe, though it still makes furniture of the highest quality, is also a growing centre for modern technology. There is a museum in Castle Hill House with a collection of old chairs and chair-making equipment.

The Guildhall is said to be the scene of one of High Wycombe's most interesting ancient customs. Each year after mayor making, the incoming and outgoing mayors are solemnly weighed to make sure that neither gets fat at the rate-payers' expense during his year of office — an idea that might with profit be extended to other

public servants.

Hughenden Manor Originally a plain brick 18th century house, Hughenden Manor was bought by Benjamin Disraeli, the flamboyant Victorian statesman, in 1847 at the beginning of his parliamentary career. It was dramatically remodelled for him by the architect E. B. Lamb in 1862 in a pretended and rather pretentious 'Jacobean' style. Angled brickwork was added wherever possible, stepped battlements were set out along all parapets and diagonally-placed pinnacles adorned each corner. Internally compound piers supporting Gothic arches and panelled ceilings were installed even in the smallest spaces. Only the library seen here was spared Gothic improvement and allowed to retain its original fireplace and simple plastered ceiling.

Disraeli, later Lord Beaconsfield, lived at Hughenden for 33 years until his death in 1881 — he is buried in a chapel in the grounds — and during that time he became first Chancellor of the Exchequer in 1852 under Lord Derby then Prime Minister in 1868 and again in 1874. Besides his official duties, Disraeli was also a successful novelist and wrote *Lothair* (1870) and *Endymion* (1880) at Hughenden — probably at this very desk.

The Old Rectory, Beaconsfield Beaconsfield, like so many other Buckinghamshire towns in the commuter zone, has something of a split personality — the Old Town round the parish church, the 'New Town' round the railway station. Not that some of the new towns are really all that new nowadays and Beaconsfield is a case in point. The railway — the Great Western on its way to Princes Risborough and on to the Midlands — first arrived in 1862. Here, however, we are clearly near the church and in the 'Old Town' and this splendid timber-framed house — the Old Rectory — dates from c1500 but was restored in 1901 and again in 1970 as the tablets over the gate commemorate. It is one of the most important timber-framed houses in the county which has comparatively few examples of the type. It is of two storeys and is built round three sides of a courtyard with the wings extended for the purpose. The hall is in the recessed centre. The lower storey is of brick with blue headers laid in a diapered pattern. The framing of the upper storey which is jettied (ie it 'oversails' the lower) has rectangular rather than the more usual square panelling of this area. The curved diagonal braces are also quite unusual in this part of England.

The derivation of Beaconsfield's name also seems to be capable of two interpretations. Is it 'the field of the beacon' — there is certainly a Beacon Hill headland above the town — or is it, as another authority suggests, 'the field of the beeches' — there is no shortage of those either.

The Parish Church, Beaconsfield 'Ends' are a particular feature of Buckinghamshire towns and villages and Old Beaconsfield is no exception. The Parish Church stands where all the ends come together; London End, Windsor End, Wycombe End and Aylesbury End — a reminder of the town's importance as a market town and centre of communications for the Chilterns in earlier times. The market — one of the biggest and most popular in the county — is still held just outside the churchyard.

The church itself — St Mary and All Saints — is of local flint with Portland stone dressing and was virtually rebuilt by the Victorians in 1869. As usual they gilded a quite adequate Perpendicular lily of a west tower by adding a decorated parapet, battlements and pinnacles including the larger stair turret with its spirelet but they kept the original Perpendicular buttresses with their chequered pattern. The walls also show some interesting flint work including the use of squared flints inside brick panels.

The box tomb with the obelisk in the foreground is that of Edmund Waller, the Civil War poet, who died in 1687. The son of a local landowner — the Hall Barn estate — Waller became related by marriage to Cromwell. He embraced the Commonwealth cause with something less than conviction and except for his flattering verses to both Charles and Cromwell at appropriate moments might have lost his head to either of them. He also tried — rather more convincingly perhaps — to embrace Lady Dorothy Sidney, niece of the Elizabethan hero of the battle of Zutphen but she preferred an earl whom she subsequently married. It was to her that Waller addressed his most celebrated poem:

Go, Lovely Rose!
Tell her, that wastes her time and me,
That now she knows,
When I resemble her to thee,
How sweet and fair she seems to be.

42

St Mary's Church, Denham The old village of Denham is one of the most attractive in the Greater London area of which, regrettably, it now forms part. St Mary's Church seen here stands at the gate of the drive to Denham Court approaches by an avenue of lime trees. It was here that the great Jacobean poet, John Dryden wrote his celebrated *'Ode to the Feast of St Cecilia'*. The church and the Court stand at the end of Denham's often filmed main street with its charming houses, cottages and old inns.

The church tower is flint and stone and probably dates from Norman times — notice the round-headed openings on either side of the belfry. The nave contains a fascinating collection of Elizabethan Tudor monuments including a brass to Sir Edmund Peckham who was Master of the Mint to Henry VIII and a monetarist who restored the value of the currency and laid the foundations for the prosperity of the Elizabethan era. There is also a 13th century font made of Purbeck marble and a defaced but authentic 500-year old 'Doom' painting above the south doorway showing the archangel Gabriel sounding the last trump on Judgement Day with shrouded figures rising from their graves.

Friends' Meeting House, Jordans This simple brick building with its hipped roof is known throughout the Western world as the first meeting house of the Quakers and the burial place of William Penn (1644-1718) the founder of the state of Pennsylvania. The building was erected in 1688 following James II's Declaration of Indulgence which sought freedom of worship primarily for Catholics but benefited the Quakers as well. The single storey end of the building is the meeting hall with a raised dais for the elders; the two storey end comprises a dwelling house for the caretaker.

William Penn was the son of an admiral who, among other things, bequeathed to his son a debt of £16,000 owed by Charles II for money lent to him in exile. In discharge of the debt, William Penn received a grant of land in the American colonies that roughly corresponded to what is now the state of Pennsylvania. Penn was associated with the infant colony for 36 years and laid down a code of high-minded but totally impracticable principles under which it should be governed. He spent only four years there during which time he founded his city of brotherly love — Philadelphia. He is buried in the graveyard here with his two wives.

Another grave is that of Thomas Ellwood, a contemporary of Penn's, who started the Quaker custom of refusing to remove his hat in deference to anyone other than God.

Milton's Cottage, Chalfont St Giles Milton was growing old in lonelineness and blindness in London in 1665, the Plague year. An ardent supporter of Cromwell and the Commonwealth, he had been discredited at the Restoration which left him friendless. At one time he was arrested and fined: at another he saw all his books burnt by the common hangman. He was at work on *Paradise Lost* — he dictated to his daughter — which is said to have been inspired by the Quaker family, the Penningtons of Chalfont St Peter. It was their tutor Thomas Ellwood — who now lies beside them and William Penn at Jordans — who found this 'pretty box' for Milton and his family to gain refuge from the plague. If *Paradise Lost* reflects Milton's disillusion he was inspired by this cottage despite his blindness to begin *Paradise Regained*. (It is said that one day Thomas Ellwood, after reading Milton's manuscripts said to him: 'Thou hast said much here of Paradise lost, but what hast thou to say of Paradise found?')

Amersham Old Town The old town of Amersham lies in the valley of the Misborne and is an ancient settlement. Amersham-on-the-Hill is recent. The first owes its existence to the medieval track from London to Aylesbury through the Wendover gap; the other grew up along the railway track when the Metropolitan line was extended from Little Chalfont in 1892.

Dominating the old town is the parish church of St Mary with its distinctive west tower — note the stair turret with its spirelet — which enjoyed external restoration in 1890. Some of its structure, however, dates back at least until the 13th century and there are monuments as early as 1430 in the nave. There is also, on the north side, a chapel of memorials to members of the Drake family from Shardeloes. To the right of the church is the Market Hall with its white-painted cupola — built for the town by the Drake family. A fair held in September in the street alongside the Market Hall was originally granted by King John (d 1216) no doubt as a part of a royal fund-raising scheme. Later, during the martyr-burning years, one of them, William Tylsworth was burnt in Amersham, his daughter, it is said, being forced to light the faggots. In 1553 John Knox preached against Mary Tudor from the pulpit of the parish church and a century later Richard Baxter 'conducted a controversy with soldiers of Cromwell's army from the same pulpit, from morning until evening hearing, he said, 'an abundance of nonsense'.

Chesham The River Chess cuts a deep valley in the dip slope of the Chilterns and flows south eastwards into Hertfordshire at Chenies. At its source stands Chesham, an ancient town who origins go back to Saxon times on a site where the Romans had an earlier settlement. Despite its development as part of the Metropolitan Railways' 'Metroland', much of Old Chesham, as here at The Bury, still retains a village atmosphere. The church in the background with its recessed lead spire is St Mary's and stands in the grounds of Chesham Park. It is in flint with a 'puddingstone' base and although it has retained a number of its Norman and medieval features — notably its two storeyed Perpendicular south porch — it suffered a massive restoration in 1869 at the hands of Sir Gilbert Scott and at the expense of the Duke of Bedford.

Chesham once had its own 'Mad Hatter', Roger Crab a haberdasher who was one of the most extraordinary characters of the 17th century. He was condemned by Cromwell, pardoned and released to become a vegetarian hermit, drinking nothing but water and wearing only sackcloth. He was the author of 'The English Hermite or the Wonder of this Age'. He died in 1680.

Hampden House, Great Hampden This is the ancestral home of the Hampden family whose greatest son was the Puritan John Hampden who, as his 19th century memorial put it:

> For these lands in Stoke Mandeville John Hampden was assessed in 20s ship money levied by the command of the king without authority of law on the 4th of August 1635. By resisting the claim of the king in legal strife he upheld the right of the people under the law and became entitled to grateful remembrance.

John Hampden's action exacerbated the struggle between king and parliament which led to the Civil War which in turn cost Hampden his life. He died of wounds at Chalgrove 'fight' in nearby Oxfordshire in 1643 but the cause of his death remains uncertain. Some say he was hit by a Royalist musket ball that shattered his shoulder, others that his own over-charged pistol exploded in his hand. Arthur Mee records that one of Hampden's 19th-century biographers, Lord Nugent, dug up the body in the local church but could find no proof either way.

The architectural history of the house stretches from before John Hampden's time — possibly as early as the 14th century — until well after it. The biggest change was that brought about by his descendants, the Earls of Buckinghamshire who enlarged the house in the mid 18th century in an early example of the Gothic revival.

Princes Risborough This ancient market town guards one of the gaps carved in the Chiltern escarpment by the melt water of the glacier of the last Ice Age. The main focus of the town is its market square and this quaint Market Hall. It was built in 1824 on the site on an earlier market hall and is of local brick with wooden posts supporting its lean-to roofs. Princes Risborough was an important railway junction at the turn of the century for besides the mainline routes to Oxford, Birmingham and the Great Central to Rugby, it was the junction of branches to Aylesbury and Watlington. Thus most of the development of the town is late 19th and early 20th century but at its centre it still has a number of interesting 18th century houses.

The name 'Risborough' is Old English for a scrub covered hillside and the term 'Princes' stems from the town's long association with the Duchy of Cornwall. The first Duke of Cornwall was Edward, Prince of Wales — better known as the 'Black Prince' had a castle here but little remains except a few stones and earthworks.

'Cymbeline's Mount' from Coombe Hill

Along the escarpment of the Chilterns there are a number of Iron Age hill forts and burial mounds. The typical flat-topped chalk spur seen here is in the grounds of Chequers and is by tradition believed to have been used by Cymbeline the Ancient British king who held sway following the first Roman invasion in 55BC. He reigned from 5AD to c40AD and was sufficiently ingratiated with the Romans to engrave his coinage with the words *'Rex Britannicus'*. (Shakespeare based a play on some of the legend.) The nearby village of Great Kimble claims that its name is a corruption of Cymbeline which just to make the argument thoroughly circular means in itself, 'cyne belle' or 'royal-hill'.

This photograph was taken from Coombe Hill near Ellesborough, another National Trust property and a favourite viewpoint — at 852ft (255m) the highest point in the Chilterns — given to the Trust in 1918 by Lord and Lady Lee of Fareham.

Ellesborough See here from the slopes of Cymbelline's Mount, is Ellesborough with its distinctive tall church tower with its even taller stair turret. The village stands on an outcrop of Chiltern chalk and has commanding views over Aylesbury and the Vale and southwards along the escarpment. The church is dedicated to St Peter and St Paul and although it has some 14th century features it is, externally, nearly all Victorian. The church contains a portrait brass of Thomas Hawtrey in Tudor armour and it was he who built the Tudor mansion at Chequers Court which is now the Prime Minister's official country residence. The house belonged to the Hawtrey family for 350 years and stands in a combe in the Chilterns above Ellesborough. It was given to the nation in 1917 by Lord Lee of Farnham 'as a thank-offering for her deliverance in the Great War and as a place of rest and recreation for her Prime Ministers for ever'. Judging by the number of urgent conferences which from time to time are held there, and the number of important decisions that have been taken there in peace and war, 'rest and recreation' for prime ministers is purely relative. The offer was also nearly turned down by the cabinet of the day. Some members thought the house too grand for prime ministers drawn from the middle classes.

Wendover In a superb setting at the foot of the Chiltern escarpment under Boddington Hill and one of the highest points — Coombe Hill (850ft, 254m) — Wendover commands one of the major gaps in the hill range created, it is believed, by melt water at the end of the last Ice Age. Along this valley run the major communications with London, the former Metropolitan line that made the town a suburb, '... Wendover, a gem of rural scenery' said the Metroland publicity; and the main London to Aylesbury road, an old highway that crosses the much more ancient Icknield Way in the centre of the town. Not far from this junction at the top of the High Street stands the clock tower depicted here. Built in 1842 it once housed the town's lock-up in its brick base.

During the autumn of 1914, the wooded hill of Halton became the site of a huge training camp for 20,000 soldiers and the Metropolitan Railway advertised special excursions for 'all those desirous of witnessing the making of an army.' A branch line to Halton Camp was built by German prisoners of war in 1917 and remained in use when Halton was developed by the Royal Air Force as a training school for the highest skilled among its technicians. The line

closed in 1963.

Pitstone Green Mill near Ivinghoe The oldest post mill in Buckinghamshire and probably one of the oldest in Britain, Pitstone Green Mill has timbers dating back to 1627. It was virtually derelict when it came into the hands of the National Trust in 1963 but it has been restored with great care and skill and is now open to the public from May to September. The National Trust also owns the Ashridge Estate of which Ivinghoe Beacon in the background is part. Commanding superb views over the surrounding countryside, this 760ft (240m) hill was an important fort in prehistoric times and finds made during excavations there have helped to date the opening phases of the Iron Age in Britain to the 6th or 7th centuries BC. The name is also of interest. Local legend, according to Arthur Mee, suggests that Sir Walter Scott may have taken the name of his famous novel from Ivinghoe after hearing a local vernacular jingle about John Hampden's celebrated gesture against the imposition of 'Ship Money'.

> *Tring, Wing and Ivanhoe*
> *Hampden of Hampden did forego*
> *For striking of ye Prince a blow*
> *And glad he might escapen so*

64

Aylesbury: The County Hall Because of its location in the middle of the county and its importance as a centre for road, rail and canal links, Aylesbury has been the 'county town' of Buckinghamshire since Tudor times and the seat of the Assizes. It has undergone considerable development in recent years largely as a result of an agreement between the county council and several London boroughs to receive 'overspill'. Despite the inevitable expansion of the town it has still been able to retain in parts the features and atmosphere of what Pevsner called 'a market town, prosperous in the 18th century.'

One example is the old County Hall, completed in 1740 to a design approved by Sir John Vanbrugh. (It was replaced, at least in function, in the 1960s by an 11 storey tower block designed by F. B. Pooley and approved by the Concrete Society.) A particular feature is the court room on the first floor which despite a serious fire in 1970 has been carefully restored as an almost perfect 18th century room with box-pews, galleries and a raised judge's seat complete with receptacle for the judge's chamber pot.

The statue guarded by lions and facing into Market Square is of the third Lord Chesham (d 1907) who, inter alia, owned 12,000 acres of the county.

Aylesbury: Church Street One of the streets that reflects Aylesbury's earlier role as a prosperous market town, Church Street is a microcosm of English domestic architecture. All the houses across the road from the Museum were probably timber framed and of 16th century origin like the one on the right. The house opposite with its frilly bargeboards and decorative hood moulds was refronted in stucco c1840. The house to its right with the pedimented doorcase was refronted in brick perhaps a hundred years earlier.

The Museum itself is housed in two buildings, the Grammar School built in 1719 and the early 18th century Ceeley House whose Corinthian portico is visible on the left. The Museum is the headquarters of the distinguished Buckinghamshire Archaeological Society.

68

Cuddington This ancient village stands on the top of a limestone ridge overlooking the valley of the River Thame as it runs southwestwards through the Vale of Aylesbury to join the Thames in Oxfordshire. This is 'wychert' country where a mixture of chalky marl and straw rather akin to West Country cob is used to build walls lining the village lanes. Like cob, wychert needs a 'good hat and a stout pair of shoes' and is usually mounted on a limestone plinth and thatched or tiled on top. The village is renowned for its cottages, timber framed with white washed plaster infilling sitting under deep eaved thatch — there is a superb example in the the background.

The church, St Nicholas, is of local limestone as are the churchyard walls. It dates from the 12th century and is of considerable interest to antiquarians because of its arcades. Like so many other Bucks churches, it was heavily restored in the 19th century and the architect responsible was G. E. Street who was very active in the county.

Haddenham 'Wychert' walls, plinthed and tiled or thatched, are features of Haddenham which in earlier times was a centre for duck-rearing to supply 'Aylesbury ducks from Bucks' and had a number of ponds for the purpose. It was also the butt of many local jokes one of which was that the thatched walls so enclosed one pond that the villagers were said to have thatched it to keep the ducks dry. Another but grimmer joke was that they put up gates to keep the plague out.

Haddenham is another of the Buckinghamshire 'long' villages where a long crooked high street links together a number of 'ends' — called 'diggs' — without a real village centre. And the 'ends' rejoice in a variety of happy names: Dragon's Tail, Rosemary Lane, Stockwell Furlong and Dollicott are but a few.

Long Crendon This large spreading but picturesque hill top village has origins going back to Roman times if not earlier and takes its name from 'Creodun' — or 'Creoda's hill' — after the son of the first king of the West Saxons. The 'Long' comes from the winding high street that links together a series of groups of cottages forming the familiar Buckinghamshire 'ends'.

In the 19th century the village was a centre for the cottage industry of needle-making until the mechanisation implicit in the Industrial Revolution saw it transferred to Redditch. Lacemaking was also a village industry until about 1900.

Long Crendon is a conservation area — it has over one hundred buildings of special architectural and historical interest including the 16th century Court House seen here on the left of the photograph. Although Arthur Mee says that it was given by Henry V to his bride, Katherine of France, after Agincourt in 1415, most of the building is of a later date. It has served many purposes in its time. It was once a hall for wool merchants setting the 'staple' (ie the price) of wool. At another time it served as a meeting place for the Warden and scholars of All Souls College, Oxford founded as a charity for singing masses for the soul of Henry V. Later it served as a court house for the church. It was nearly demolished by Church Commissioners in 1890 but was one of the first buildings to be bought — and saved — by the National Trust in 1900. It is open to the public.

St Mary's church in the background is of Norman origin substantially rebuilt in the 13th century. The 'Perpendicular' upper part of the crossing tower with its stair turret was added in the 16th century.

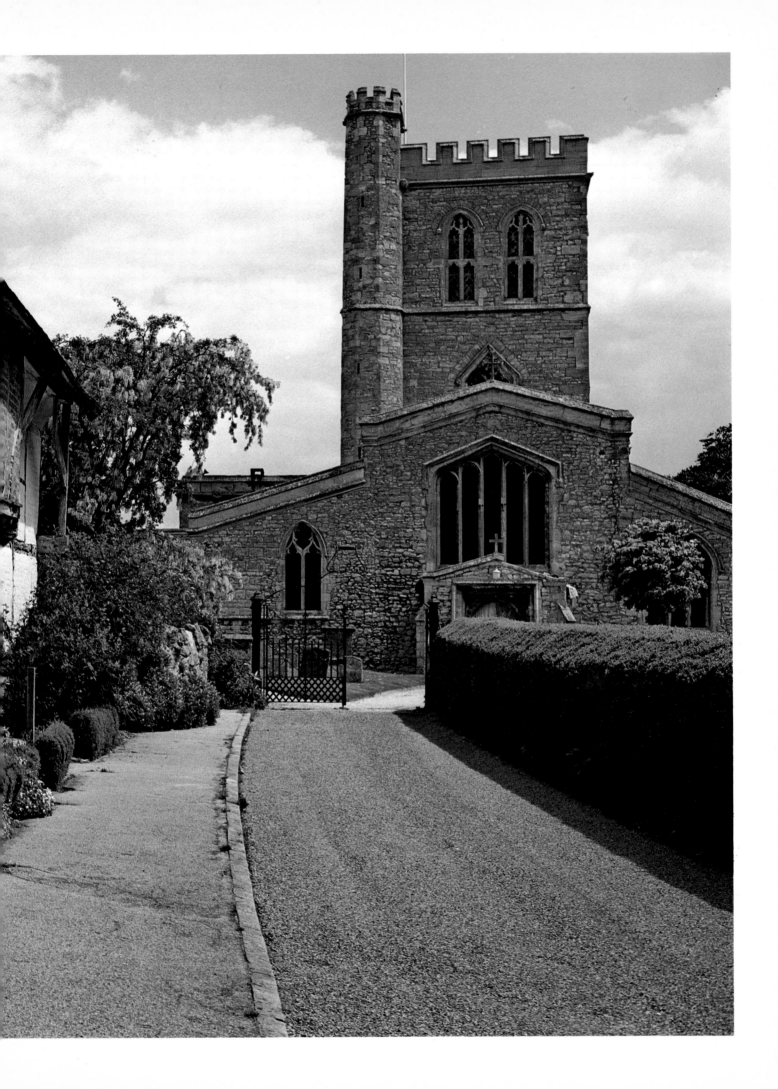

Brill Common and Windmill As is evident here, Brill commands splendid views deep into Oxfordshire and must therefore have been an observation post of value to both sides in the Civil War. Although the 'front' between the Royalists based at Oxford and the Cromwellians at Aylesbury ran through this area for much of the war and there was much skirmishing and advance and retreat, the diggings on Brill Common are only partly attributable to military purposes. Most of them are the result of clay workings over several centuries — Brill is another of the familiar limestone 'outliers' but is capped with clay. Tiles, bricks and primitive pots are made in the district from the 13th century onwards. As recently as Victorian times there were as many as seven active potteries mostly making plant-pot earthenware.

The windmill is a post-mill — the main chamber with all its gears and millstones could be rotated to suit the direction of the wind. It is thus of light timber framing with weather boarding. The base is more substantially built of brick. The mill carries the date of 1668, is now owned by the Buckinghamshire County Council and is open to the public at week-ends.

Until 1936 an extension of the railway from Quainton Road ran to a terminus on the north side of the hill and was known as 'the Wotton tramway.'

Boarstall Tower All that remains of a 14th century moated house in the depths of the then extensive Bernewood Forest, Boarstall Tower reflects many periods of history in its architecture. A licence to crenellate — a sort of medieval planning permission — was granted in 1312 in the reign of Edward II. Later the house was occupied by both sides during the Civil War and finally fell to the Parliamentarians under Fairfax in 1646 who, as was usual with such fortified places, 'slighted' it. The surviving gatehouse was substantially altered later in the 17th century as the mullioned and transomed windows reveal. It became the home of the Aubrey family for many generations and was given to the National Trust by the Aubrey-Fletchers in 1942. It is, however, let by the Trust and is not open to the public.

Waddesdon Manor   Baron Ferdinand de Rothschild (1839-98), a grandson of the founder of the Austrian branch of the great banking house, settled in England in 1860 and bought the Waddesdon estate from the Duke of Marlborough in 1874. He had the top of the hill levelled and fully grown trees planted around the site and then built Waddesdon Manor in the style of a French Renaissance château similar to those at Chambord and Blois. His architect was Hippolyte Alexander Gabriel Walter Destailleur (1822-93) who created what Pevsner calls 'an utter surprise in its Chiltern setting'. Work was completed in 1880 but there was a further extension in 1889 by Destailleur junior.

Baron Ferdinand was a great admirer of French 18th century art and he built up an immense collection of furniture, paintings and porcelain. But he was by no means exclusive in his taste — despite the flamboyant baroque of the Manor — and he also built up a collection of fine English 18th century portraits and paintings by earlier Dutch and Flemish masters. At his death, Waddesdon and most of his collection passed to his sister Miss Alice de Rothschild. She was also a collector — of arms and armour and Sèvres and Meissen china. When she died in 1922 Waddesdon and its artistic contents passed to Mr James de Rothschild who again added to the collection. When he died in 1957 he bequeathed the house and the combined collections to the National Trust. The house and its gardens are now open to the public from late March to October.

This view of the garden front of the mansion and the fountain in the foreground is said to be Italian dating from the 17th century but Pevsner feels it more likely to have been 19th century.

The Morning Room, Waddesdon Manor
The Morning Room was part of the extension carried out by Destailleur junior in 1889, and this photograph gives us a glimpse of the splendour of the treasures the house contains. Above the fireplace is a portrait by Sir Joshua Reynolds (d 1792) of *Emily Pott depicted as Thais* — a 17th century actress not inappropriately portraying an Athenian courtesan. To the right are two paintings by Dutch masters — *A view of the Maas* by Albert Cuyp (d 1691) and beneath it *The Tete a Tete* by Gabriel Metsu (d 1667), a further landscape by Cuyp and two pictures by the celebrated Dutch painter of seascapes, Willem van der Velde, the younger, (d 1707). Next to the door is a portrait by Gainsborough painted in 1786 and beneath it another landscape of the 17th century Dutch school this time by Philips Wouverman (d 1668).

The furniture is largely French. The large black lacquer secretaire by the door was made in France c1770 and the black writing table in the foreground carries a bronze equestrian statuette of Louis XIV. The two striking blue vases are for pot pourri and were made of Chinese celadon — a semi-translucent glaze — and mounted in French ormulu c1745-9. All the chairs are covered in Beauvais tapestry.

Almshouses, Quainton Once destined by the grandiose but happily unrealised dreams of Sir Edwin Watkin the 19th century chairman of the old Metropolitan Railway to become, as John Betjeman put it, 'the Crewe of Buckinghamshire', Quainton remains largely unspoilt. Its only connection with the railway is Quainton Road station a mile away in the valley which now houses a railway museum of growing importance.

Quainton was the birthplace of the county's first great historian, George Lipscomb. He was born in 1773 and his *History of Buckinghamshire* was published in 1847 but he died a year earlier, in a London garret, exhausted and penniless after the years he had devoted to the book.

The Winwood Almshouses on the right of the photograph date from 1687 and are pre-classical in style. Of particular interest are the diagonally placed chimney stacks, the way in which the dormer windows alternate with bigger and smaller gables and the Dutch gables over the porches. They were built by Richard Winwood (d 1689) who was the son of the Secretary of State to James I. He lived in Quainton Manor — now part of Denham Lodge north-east of the village — and is commemorated with his wife by a magnificent monument in the nearby church clad in armour and wearing a wig with his wife kneeling beside him.

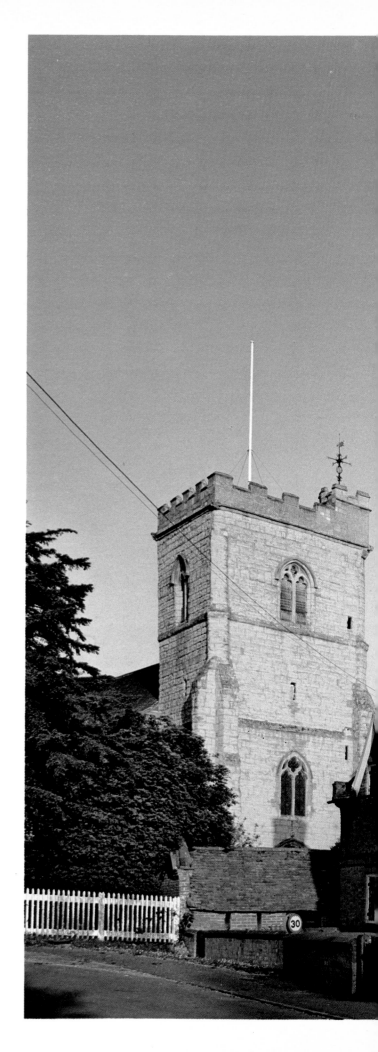

The view south from Quainton Hill One of the limestone outliers that characterise this part of the county, Quainton Hill rises to 600ft (187m) and is the highest point in the centre of Buckinghamshire. The village tumbles down the slope of the hill on the left and its austere brown brick tower mill without sails — first built c1830 and restored in 1976 — is clearly visible. There are splendid views form the top of the hill and it is said that in clear weather the Shropshire hills can be seen. Looking south in this photograph, the main feature is the Waddesdon ridge in the right middle ground. The ridge was bare when Waddesdon Manor was built on it in 1874. Its top was flattened and Baron de Rothschild had a narrow gauge steam railway built from Quainton Road station to carry horse-drawn wagons loaded with stone for the house and fully grown trees for the park.

Ascott near Wing   This is another Rothschild mansion bought in 1874 by Leopold de Rothschild as a family hunting lodge and a home for the Rothschild staghounds. The house is timber-framed and carries the date of 1606 over its main doorway. It was originally the family home of the Dormers, a prominent Buckinghamshire family in Tudor times commemorated in Wing by Dormer's Hospital founded in 1569. The Rothschilds had the house enlarged in the same style in the 19th century and again in 1938. The house was presented to the National Trust in 1949 and as the Guide puts it 'Ascott is one of the few country houses accepted by the Trust on other than architectural merits.' The 'other merits' were the gardens which extend for 30 acres and were laid out at the end of the last century by Sir Harry Veitch, the celebrated Chelsea horticulturist, and the house's magnificent contents which rival those of nearby Waddesdon. They include both French and English furniture and a collection of pictures by Rubens, Hogarth, Gainsborough and Hobbema as well as late-period Turners. Of particular interest is Anthony de Rothschild's collection of Chinese porcelain. The house is open to the public from April to the end of September.

The elaborate fountains in the foreground is part of the formal French garden. Its sculptor, an American called Ralph Waldo Story lived in Paris and had a penchant for naked naiads and cockleshell chariots drawn by sea horses. He did a similar fountain for Lord Astor at Cliveden.

Stewkley A long thin village — over a mile between its north and south 'ends' — Stewkley was once a centre for straw plaiting, a cottage industry producing material for a host of items but especially straw hats. When the hat trade declined, Stewkley with its rather remote location — it has no railway station and away from main roads — became neglected. This may be one of the reasons why its ancient church — Pevsner says it is the 'most splendid piece of Norman architecture in Buckinghamshire' — escaped the attentions of the more virulent 19th century 'scrapers'. Of particular interest is the sumptuous use of the traditional Norman zig-zag motif in decoration not just of the door and window arches, as is usual, but in the form of a string course running right round the church, and on the tower arches. Notice too the round window. The small windows and the multiple arches of the west door — notice the two lunettes cut out of the strangely shaped tympanum above the door — are all evidence of Norman origin. Pevsner dates the church between 1140-1150.

Stewkley itself has some interesting 16th and 17th century timber-framed buildings. One of them, Manor Farmhouse, has a dovecote with diapered brickwork and dated 1704 which could accommodate 800 pigeons. At the North End there is some evidence of a Civil War skirmish and in more recent times Stewkley, with its neighbours Wing and Cublington, was involved in another skirmish — this time against being chosen as the site of a third London airport. Had they lost, this church despite its Norman origins would no doubt have fallen victim to a more deadly form of latter day scraper.

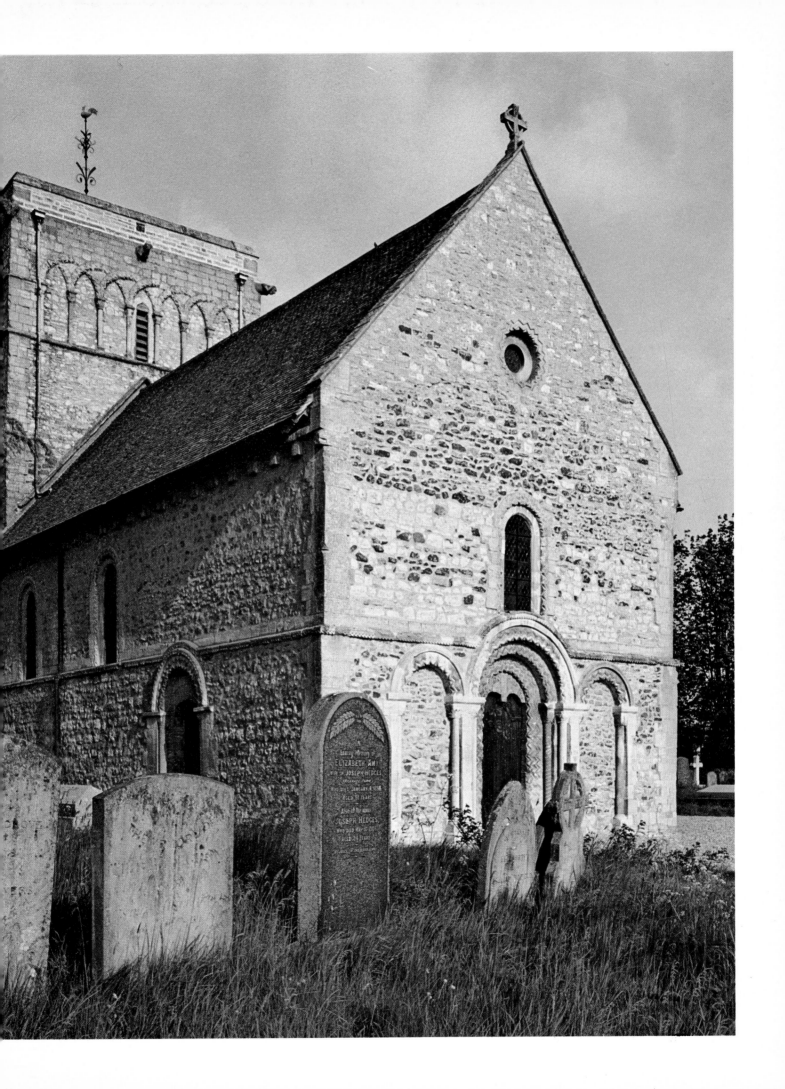

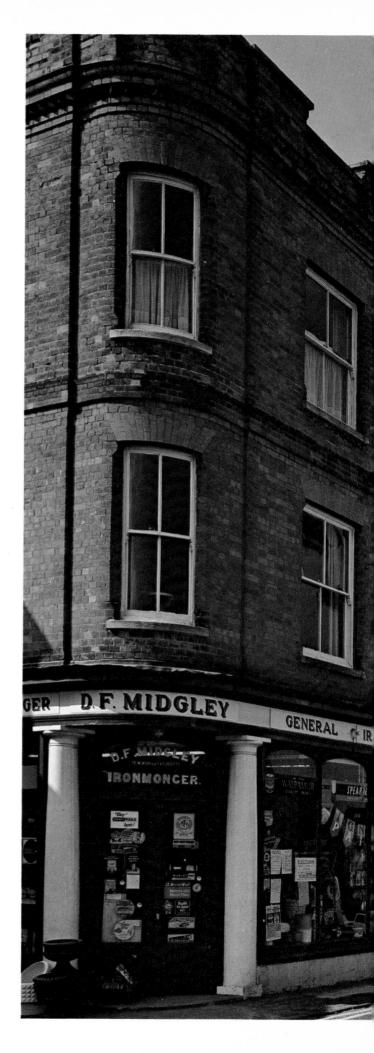

Winslow This handsome market town has a history that goes back to Offa, the 8th century Saxon king of Mercia, who besides building Offa's Dyke from the Severn to the Dee, gave Winslow to St Alban's Abbey c780AD as the 'fairest jewel in his crown'. The centre of the town is its attractive market square with two antique hostelries — the Bell Hotel on the south side and the one shown here, the 18th century George Hotel on the southwest corner. (The 'George' depicted on the inn sign looks rather more like the Duke of Wellington than any of the later Hanoverians.) More interesting is the splendidly ornate wrought iron balcony. It might have come from Cheltenham; in fact it came from Claydon House no doubt in payment for some outstanding debt.

Winslow Hall Built for William Lowndes, Secretary of the Treasury during Queen Anne's reign who, among other things, helped to bring about a stabilising of the value of the coinage — monetarism is not a purely 20th century phenomenon — Winslow House stands on the site of the former Winslow Manor which Lowndes acquired in 1700. He was an outstanding public servant and after his death Lord Chesterfield said of him 'Old Mr Lowndes, the famous Secretary of the Treasury used to say — 'Take care of the pence and the pounds will take care of themselves' — thereby giving currency to a new English proverb. Lowndes undoubtedly applied his principle as much to his personal as to his public affairs and became an extremely wealthy man. (In 1712 he also built The Bury at Chesham.) One of his close associates was Sir Christopher Wren and evidence suggests that it was Wren who was responsible for the design of the house rather than Inigo Jones who has been credited with it. Certainly Wren kept an eye on the accounts. The house is of local red and grey brick and the woodwork was completed by the royal joiner and the gardens by the royal gardener. It typifies the elegant restraint of both the period and the architect and is one of the oustanding buildings in Buckinghamshire.

Claydon House, Middle Claydon The old manor house here, already historic, was bought by Sir Ralph Verney, Lord Mayor of London in 1465 and with not a few vicissitudes, the Verney family has lived here ever since. One Verney, Sir Francis (d 1615) was a pirate. Another, the Puritan Sir Edmund, after 30 years' royal service but against his conscience remained loyal to King Charles I on the outbreak of the Civil War. He became the King's standard bearer and died at the battle of Edgehill in 1642 still clutching the standard so tightly that his hand had to be hacked off. (His ghost is said to appear at Claydon whenever the family is threatened.) He was succeeded by Sir Ralph Verney, a Parliamentarian, whose son later became the 1st Baron Verney. The 2nd Baron Verney rebuilt the house from the 1750s to the 1780s intending that it should rival in splendour the mansion of the Temples at Stowe. It broke him. When he went bankrupt in 1784 virtually two thirds of the house was pulled down by his creditors who stripped everything that was moveable from doorframes and mantelpieces to wrought iron balconies.

The south wing was left more or less undamaged and it contains the most heavily decorated rooms of the original house. One of them is this dazzling Chinese room of which Pevsner says: 'the climax of the Chinese room is an alcove encrusted with rococo chinoiserie carved with extreme boldness and gusto'.

In Victorian times, Sir Henry Verney (he adopted the name after marrying the earl's niece) restored the family fortunes and the house was remodelled in 1860. Sir Henry later married the sister of Florence Nightingale and Florence herself spent her later years at Claydon.

The house was given to the National Trust in 1956 by the Verney family who continue to live in it. It is open to the public from April to October.

The Town Hall, Buckingham Although Buckingham was made the county town in 888AD by King Alfred the Great, its position in the northwest corner of the county made it unsuitable as a centre for administration — especially that of justice. In consequence by Tudor times the county assizes had been transferred to the more centrally placed Aylesbury. The Assizes were returned to Buckingham in 1708 but a serious fire destroyed much of the town in 1725 and the County Hall was built in Aylesbury in 1740. Buckingham then became what it has remained — an historic and very attractive market town and bearing the name and the arms of its ancient county.

Those arms — a golden swan in chains — are visible here surmounting the clock tower. They were given to the town — and the county — by the Giffards, a Norman family who built a castle here — now the site of the parish church — shortly after the Conquest. The Town Hall itself dominates the market place. It is a late 17th century building refronted in red brick in 1780.

Stowe A house of national — even international importance — as a splendid example of 18th century English domestic architecture and landscape design at its best, Stowe and its great park stand at the end of a three-mile avenue of trees leading from Buckingham.

The first important house to be built on the site in 1680 was, like so many other houses of the period in Buckinghamshire, part of an upsurge of building country mansions and establishing estates that followed the Restoration. It was a brick built house with a hipped roof, a balustrade, and stone quoins in the Wren manner and is still part of the massive north front of the existing house. Its builder was the 3rd Baronet, Sir Richard Temple. The 4th baronet — also Sir Richard — who inherited in 1697 was a successful general who married the daughter of a rich brewer. He was in temporary disgrace between 1710 and 1714 and began improvements to the house and garden employing Sir John Vanbrugh (d 1726), the architect of Castle Howard ('Brideshead') in Yorkshire and of Blenheim Palace in Oxfordshire. He was made Viscount Chobham in 1718 when restored to favour and continued what was to become a lifelong task in developing his property. By 1724 it was being described as 'the finest seat in England'. Lord Chobham died in 1749. He was succeeded by his nephew Richard Grenville, a gifted amateur architect and pioneer of the Classical revival school which was then gaining in popularity. He continued the great work begun by his uncle and the designing of the Greek temples that adorn the gardens, is attributed to him. He probably had the help of William Kent. The Palladian bridge seen here is in keeping with the contemporary taste for classical structures. It is from a design by Palladio that was used by the 9th Earl of Pembroke — another gifted amateur — to build a bridge at Wilton House in 1737. Visitors from Stowe so admired it that they built a copy. There is another copy at Prior Park, Bath.

Richard Grenville became Earl Temple, his son became the Marquis of Buckingham and his grandson, the Duke of Buckingham and Chandos. The embellishment of Stowe continued and at various times Robert Adam (d 1792), Sir John Soane (d 1837) and an Italian architect Giovanni Battista Borra (d c1783) were employed on improving the house and Lancelot ('Capability') Brown served as gardener for more than 10 years.

Stony Stratford For most of its long history Stony Stratford was a small market town and staging post on the Holyhead Road — the Roman Watling Street — which forms its High Street. This broad High Street is a mile long and there are many red brick Georgian houses including two inns which have left their mark on the language — the Cock and the Bull — the home of the stories too tall to be believed — stories told and subsequently spread, with the phrase itself, by coachmen with the Irish Mail. A less cheerful story is that the ill-fated king Edward V, aged 13 and on his way to London to be crowned in 1483, stayed the night at an inn in Stony Stratford High Street where he was seized by his uncle, the Duke of Gloucester, later Richard III, and never seen again. As Arthur Mee reminds us, Shakespeare in his *Richard III* has the Archbishop of York say to Edward's mother who looked forward to seeing her son again — a meeting doomed never to take place — the following lines:-

Last night, I hear, they lay at
   Northampton;
At Stony Stratford do they lay tonight;
Tomorrow, or next day, they will be here.

The town suffered two disastrous fires in the 18th century, the second destroying the eastern half of the town and one of its churches.

This charming corner of the town — again with attractive Georgian houses — is Horsefair Green which once saw a roaring trade in horses, as its name implies.

Willen Church This important Wren-style church was built at the expense of one of those cheerfully sadistic public school head-masters, the great Dr Busby of Westminster School, who birched knowledge into the youth of England for more than half the 17th century. An uncompromising Royalist he held his position right through the Commonwealth and grew rich on royal rewards after the Restoration. In keeping with what was a national trend at the time he aspired to join the landed gentry and acquired the manor of Willen and had the church built at his own expense in 1680. The architect was Robert Hooke, one of his former pupils and a friend of Sir Christopher Wren. He also installed a library in the church and supplied it with plate and provided an endowment in his will.

The church is very similar to a Wren City church — similar in detail to St Mary-le-Bow — and its tower has pinnacles topped with pineapples. The apse was added in 1862 and happily is much in keeping with the 17th century church. The ceiling plasterwork, the pews with their carved ends and the font with its ogee shaped cover are all original. The font was designed by Bates who also worked for Wren.

Great Linford   Set amid the rather raw new housing of Buckinghamshire's latest 'new' town, Milton Keynes, Great Linford is being specifically preserved as a link with a more tasteful and picturesque past. The village comprises the traditional group of manor house, church and rectory with the almshouses seen here across the manorial fishpond. The almshouses were built in the late 17th century by another wealthy Restoration public figure bent on founding a manorial dynasty — Sir William Pritchard. He was a City merchant and became Lord Mayor in 1682. He created controversy by refusing to accept elected sheriffs — an action that made him popular with the Royalists but which was indirectly responsible for the celebrated Rye House Plot which almost led to a renewed Civil War.

The Almshouses are of brick and are single storey dwellings on either side of a two storey centre piece which served as a schoolhouse. (Notice the double curved gable, typical of the period.)

106

Newport Pagnell Now better known as an expanding and rather garish new town and staging post on the M1, Newport Pagnell seen here across the quiet water meadows of the River Ouse still looks like the peaceful Midlands market town it was for centuries before the motorway was built.

During the Civil War it was a central garrison for Parliament drawing levies from a considerable area and training them for battle. One such recruit is believed to have been the 16-year old John Bunyan, future author of *Pilgrim's Progress*, who came from the village of Elstow near Bedford — an archetypal English nonconformist.

Cromwell himself lost his second son, Oliver at Newport Pagnell — he died of smallpox in 1644 whilst serving as a captain with the garrison.

The parish church, seen here from the north, is SS Peter and Paul and is the largest church in this part of the county. It is largely 14th century but the broad tower was built between 1542 and 1548. The pinnacles are, however, not contemporary but a Victorian embellishment.

Olney This photograph is taken from the Clifton Reynes bluff overlooking the water meadows of the River Ouse with the pleasant stone town of Olney beyond. This is the extreme northern end of Buckinghamshire and Olney stands on the great Jurassic limestone belt that runs up from the Cotswolds to the Humber. Its church has a tall steeple atop a tall tower — the highest in Buckinghamshire that is in its original 14th century form.

Olney is known as the home of the poet William Cowper during the happiest years of his rather troubled life. He was brought here in 1767 by a remarkable clergyman, the Revd John Newton who collaborated with Cowper to produce the 'Olney Hymns' which include such classics as *Glorious Things of Thee are Spoken* and *Amazing Grace*. Cowper is best remembered for his ballad *'John Gilpin'* (1782) and for his poem *The Task* (1784) which contains the following comfortable verse:

> *Now stir the fire, and close the shutters fast,*
> *Let fall the curtains, wheel the sofa round,*
> *And, while the bubbling and loud-hissing urn*
> *Throws up a steamy column, and the cups,*
> *That cheer but not inebriate, wait on each,*
> *So let us welcome cheerful ev'ning in.*

How well Cowper suits Buckinghamshire!

There is a Cowper and Newton Museum at Cowper's former home, Orchard Side in the Market Place and it is open most days during the summer.

Index of Plates